M000028096

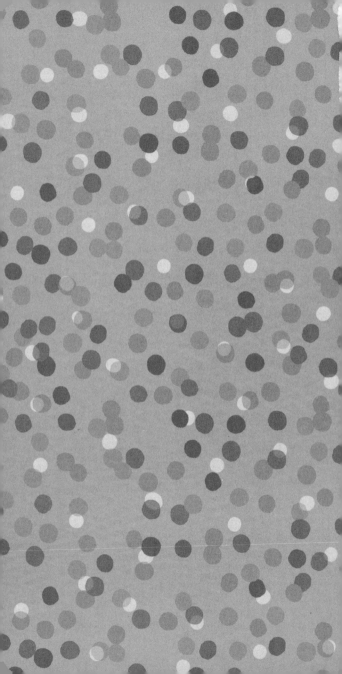

GRADUATE

Congratulations on your wonderful achievement!

May God's promises
remain with you to
encourage and guide you
through life's journey.

Promises from God for Graduates

© 2012 Christian Art Gifts, RSA
        Christian Art Gifts Inc., IL, USA

First edition 2012
Second edition 2013
Third edition 2015
Forth edition 2018

Designed by Christian Art Gifts

Images used under license from Shutterstock.com

Scripture quotations marked NLT are taken from the *Holy Bible*,
New Living Translation®. Copyright © 1996, 2004, 2007 by Tyndale
House Publishers, Inc., Carol Stream, Illinois 60188.
All rights reserved.

Scripture quotations marked NIV are taken from the *Holy Bible*,
New International Version® NIV®. Copyright © 1973, 1978, 1984, 2011
by International Bible Society. Used by permission of Zondervan
Publishing House. All rights reserved.

Scripture quotations marked ESV are taken from the *Holy Bible*,
English Standard Version. Copyright © 2001 by Crossway Bibles,
a division of Good News Publishers. Used by permission.
All rights reserved.

Scripture quotations marked MSG are taken from THE MESSAGE.
Copyright © by Eugene H. Peterson, 1993, 1994, 1995, 1996, 2000,
2001, 2002 by NavPress Publishing Group. Used by permission.

Printed in China

ISBN 978-1-4321-2772-5

PROMISES FROM GOD
— FOR —
GRADUATES

Love,
The Tuckers

Christian art gifts

Contents

GOD BLESSES THE GRADUATE WITH ...

ABILITIES

In His grace, God has given us different
gifts for doing certain things well.

Romans 12:6 NLT

There are different kinds of gifts,
but the same Spirit distributes them.

1 Corinthians 12:4 NIV

Earnestly desire the higher gifts. And I
will show you a still more excellent way.

1 Corinthians 12:31 ESV

To those who use well what they
are given, even more will be given,
and they will have an abundance.

Matthew 25:29 NLT

"The master was full of praise. 'Well
done, my good and faithful servant. You
have been faithful in handling this small
amount, so now I will give you many more
responsibilities. Let's celebrate together!'"

Matthew 25:21 NLT

Abilities

God gave us a spirit not of fear but
of power and love and self-control.

2 Timothy 1:7 ESV

I have filled him with the Spirit
of God, giving him great wisdom,
ability, and expertise.

Exodus 31:3 NLT

If the ax is dull and its edge
unsharpened, more strength is needed,
but skill will bring success.

Ecclesiastes 10:10 NIV

Abilities

"You are the light of the world – like
a city on a hilltop that cannot be hidden.
No one lights a lamp and then puts it under
a basket. Instead, a lamp is placed on a
stand, where it gives light to everyone
in the house. In the same way, let your
good deeds shine out for all to see, so that
everyone will praise your heavenly Father."

Matthew 5:14-16 NLT

God has given each of you a gift from
His great variety of spiritual gifts.
Use them well to serve one another.

1 Peter 4:10 NLT

ASPIRATIONS

I press on to reach the end of the race and
receive the heavenly prize for which God,
through Christ Jesus, is calling us.

Philippians 3:14 NLT

God can do anything, you know – far more
than you could ever imagine or guess or
request in your wildest dreams!

Ephesians 3:20 MSG

Aspirations

Search for the LORD and for
His strength; continually seek Him.

1 Chronicles 16:11 NLT

The aspirations of good people
end in celebration.

Proverbs 10:28 MSG

Let your roots grow down into Him,
and let your lives be built on Him.
Then your faith will grow strong
in the truth you were taught, and
you will overflow with thankfulness.

Colossians 2:7 NLT

Aspirations

Aspire to live quietly, and to mind your
own affairs, and to work with your hands.

1 Thessalonians 4:11 ESV

Take delight in the LORD and He will
give you your heart's desires.

Psalm 37:4 NLT

Grow in the grace and knowledge of
our Lord and Savior Jesus Christ.
To Him be glory both now and forever!

2 Peter 3:18 NIV

Put God in charge of your work, then
what you've planned will take place.

Proverbs 16:3 MSG

The LORD God is a sun and shield;
the LORD bestows favor and honor.
No good thing does He withhold
from those who walk uprightly.

Psalm 84:11 ESV

"I'm on My way to the Father because the
Father is the goal and purpose of My life."

John 14:28 MSG

FREEDOM

When we died with Christ we were
set free from the power of sin.

Romans 6:7 NLT

"I've wiped the slate of all your
wrongdoings. There's nothing
left of your sins."

Isaiah 44:22 MSG

Freedom

Christ has set us free to live
a free life. So take your stand!

Galatians 5:1 MSG

"You will know the truth,
and the truth will set you free."

John 8:32 NIV

He [Jesus Christ] gave His life to free us from
every kind of sin, to cleanse us,
and to make us His very own people,
totally committed to doing good deeds.

Titus 2:14 NLT

Freedom

In my distress I prayed to the LORD, and
the LORD answered me and set me free.

Psalm 118:5 NLT

"If the Son sets you free, you are truly free."

John 8:36 NLT

All glory to Him who loves us and
has freed us from our sins by shedding
His blood for us. He has made us a
Kingdom of priests for God His Father.
All glory and power to Him
forever and ever!

Revelation 1:5-6 NLT

Freedom

You are free, yet you are God's
slaves, so don't use your freedom
as an excuse to do evil.

1 Peter 2:16 NLT

You must be careful so that your freedom
does not cause others with a weaker
conscience to stumble.

1 Corinthians 8:9 NLT

The Lord is the Spirit, and where the
Spirit of the Lord is, there is freedom.

2 Corinthians 3:17 ESV

INSPIRATION

Those who live at the ends of the
earth stand in awe of Your wonders.
From where the sun rises to where it sets,
You inspire shouts of joy.

Psalm 65:8 NLT

Blessed is the man who walks not in the
counsel of the wicked, nor stands in the way
of sinners, nor sits in the seat of scoffers;
but his delight is in the law of the LORD,
and on His law he meditates day and night.

Psalm 1:1-2 ESV

Inspiration

Carefully build yourselves up in this most holy
faith by praying in the Holy Spirit,
staying right at the center of God's love,
keeping your arms open and outstretched,
ready for the mercy of our Master,
Jesus Christ. This is the unending
life, the real life!

Jude 20-21 MSG

I remember the days of old.
I ponder all Your great works and
think about what You have done.

Psalm 143:5 NLT

Trust in the LORD with all your heart;
do not depend on your own understanding.
Seek His will in all you do,
and He will show you which path to take.

Proverbs 3:5-6 NLT

If anyone is in Christ, the new creation has come: The old has gone, the new is here!

2 Corinthians 5:17 NIV

This is the confidence we have in approaching God: that if we ask anything according to His will, He hears us.

1 John 5:14 NIV

You are the ones chosen by God, chosen for the high calling of priestly work, chosen to be a holy people, God's instruments to do His work and speak out for Him, to tell others of the night-and-day difference He made for you – from nothing to something, from rejected to accepted.

1 Peter 2:9-10 MSG

Live freely, animated and motivated
by God's Spirit. Then you won't feed
the compulsions of selfishness.

Galatians 5:16 MSG

Each of you must take responsibility
for doing the creative best you
can with your own life.

Galatians 6:5 MSG

All who seek the LORD will praise Him.
Their hearts will rejoice with everlasting joy.

Psalm 22:26 NLT

JOY

Joyful are those who live like this! Joyful indeed are those whose God is the Lord.

Psalm 144:15 NLT

You make known to me the path of life;
You will fill me with joy in Your presence,
with eternal pleasures at Your right hand.

Psalm 16:11 NIV

The LORD is my strength and shield.
I trust Him with all my heart. He helps
me, and my heart is filled with joy.
I burst out in songs of thanksgiving.

Psalm 28:7 NLT

The joy of God is your strength!

Nehemiah 8:10 MSG

Satisfy us in the morning with Your
unfailing love, that we may sing
for joy and be glad all our days.

Psalm 90:14 NIV

Joy

Rejoice in the Lord always;
again I will say, rejoice.

Philippians 4:4 ESV

Praise the Lord! How joyful are
those who fear the Lord and
delight in obeying His commands.

Psalm 112:1 NLT

I will rejoice in the Lord; I will take
joy in the God of my salvation.

Habakkuk 3:18 ESV

Joy

You make me glad by Your deeds, Lord;
I sing for joy at what Your hands have done.

Psalm 92:4 NIV

Always try to do good to each
other and to all people. Always
be joyful. Never stop praying.

1 Thessalonians 5:15-17 NLT

The Lord your God will bless you in all your
harvest and in all the work of your hands,
and your joy will be complete.

Deuteronomy 16:15 NIV

MOTIVATION

The LORD is my inheritance; therefore,
I will hope in Him! The LORD is
good to those who depend on Him,
to those who search for Him.

Lamentations 3:24-25 NLT

The LORD is my strength and my song;
He has given me victory. This is
my God, and I will praise Him –
my father's God, and I will exalt Him!

Exodus 15:2 NLT

Let yourselves be pulled into a way
of life shaped by God's life, a life
energetic and blazing with holiness.

1 Peter 1:15 MSG

With all this going for us, my dear,
dear friends, stand your ground.
And don't hold back. Throw yourselves
into the work of the Master,
confident that nothing you do for
Him is a waste of time or effort.

1 Corinthians 15:58 MSG

So let's not get tired of doing what is
good. At just the right time we will reap
a harvest of blessing if we don't give up.

Galatians 6:9 NLT

Motivation

By the grace of God I am what I am,
and His grace toward me was not in vain.

1 Corinthians 15:10 ESV

Seek His will in all you do and He
will show you which path to take.

Proverbs 3:6 NLT

You will keep in perfect peace all
who trust in You, all whose thoughts are fixed
on You! Trust in the LORD always,
for the LORD God is the eternal Rock.

Isaiah 26:3-4 NLT

Motivation

As soon as I pray, You answer me;
You encourage me by giving me strength.

Psalm 138:3 NLT

Fight the good fight of the faith. Take hold of
the eternal life to which you were called.

1 Timothy 6:12 NIV

Let us think of ways to motivate one
another to acts of love and good works.

Hebrews 10:24 NLT

"If you remain in Me and My
words remain in you, ask whatever
you wish, and it will be done for you."

John 15:7 NIV

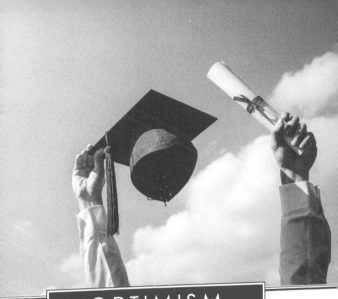

OPTIMISM

As for me, I will always have hope;
I will praise You more and more.

Psalm 71:14 NIV

What gives us hope and joy,
and what will be our proud reward
and crown as we stand before our
Lord Jesus when He returns? It is You!

1 Thessalonians 2:19 NLT

And now to Him who can keep you on your
feet, standing tall in His bright presence,
fresh and celebrating – to our one God,
our only Savior, through Jesus Christ,
our Master, be glory, majesty, strength,
and rule before all time, and now,
and to the end of all time.

Jude 24-25 MSG

Look forward to the gracious salvation
that will come to you when Jesus Christ
is revealed to the world.

1 Peter 1:13 NLT

Trust in Him at all times, O people;
pour out your heart before Him;
God is a refuge for us.

Psalm 62:8 ESV

Optimism

We don't yet see things clearly. We're
squinting in a fog, peering through a mist.
But it won't be long before the weather
clears and the sun shines bright! We'll see it
all then, see it all as clearly as God sees us,
knowing Him directly just as He knows us!

1 Corinthians 13:12 MSG

Your beauty and splendor have
everyone talking; I compose songs on
Your wonders. Your marvelous doings
are headline news; I could write a book
full of the details of Your greatness.

Psalm 145:5-6 MSG

Because of Christ and our faith
in Him, we can now come boldly and
confidently into God's presence.

Ephesians 3:12 NLT

Optimism

God is sheer beauty, all-generous
in love, loyal always and ever.

Psalm 100:5 MSG

May the God of hope fill you with all joy and
peace in believing, so that by the power of
the Holy Spirit you may abound in hope.

Romans 15:13 ESV

"Fear not, for I am with you;
be not dismayed, for I am your God;
I will strengthen you, I will help you,
I will uphold you."

Isaiah 41:10 ESV

PASSION

Never be lazy, but work hard and
serve the Lord enthusiastically.

Romans 12:11 NLT

Always work enthusiastically for
the Lord, for you know that nothing
you do for the Lord is ever useless.

1 Corinthians 15:58 NLT

Passion

It is fine to be zealous, provided the
purpose is good, and to be so always.

Galatians 4:18 NIV

Now, who will want to harm
you if you are eager to do good?

1 Peter 3:13 NLT

"Those whom I love, I reprove and
discipline, so be zealous and repent."

Revelation 3:19 ESV

Passion

Work with enthusiasm, as though you were
working for the Lord rather than for people.

Ephesians 6:7 NLT

Wait passionately for God, don't leave the
path. He'll give you your place in the sun.

Psalm 37:34 MSG

Love the LORD your God, walk in all
His ways, obey His commands,
hold firmly to Him, and serve Him
with all your heart and all your soul.

Joshua 22:5 NLT

Passion

If you search for the LORD your God with all
your heart and soul, you will find Him.

Deuteronomy 4:29 NLT

Give me an eagerness for Your
laws rather than a love for money!

Psalm 119:36 NLT

If you love the LORD your God and serve Him
with all your heart and soul, then He
will send the rains in their proper seasons.

Deuteronomy 11:13-14 NLT

Always be zealous for the fear of the LORD.

Proverbs 23:17 NIV

PEACE

In peace I will lie down and sleep, for You
alone, O LORD, will keep me safe.

Psalm 4:8 NLT

The peace of God, which transcends all
understanding, will guard your hearts and
your minds in Christ Jesus.

Philippians 4:7 NIV

Peace

Lord, You will grant us peace;
all we have accomplished is really from You.

Isaiah 26:12 NLT

The Lord bless you and keep you;
the Lord make His face shine on you
and be gracious to you; the Lord turn
His face toward you and give you peace.

Numbers 6:24-26 NIV

The Lord gives His people strength.
The Lord blesses them with peace.

Psalm 29:11 NLT

Peace

"I have said these things to you,
that in Me you may have peace.
In the world you will have tribulation.
But take heart; I have overcome the world."

John 16:33 ESV

You will keep in perfect peace
those whose minds are steadfast,
because they trust in You.

Isaiah 26:3 NIV

"Peace I leave with you; My peace
I give to you. Not as the world gives
do I give to you. Let not your hearts
be troubled, neither let them be afraid."

John 14:27 ESV

Peace

Let the peace that comes from Christ
rule in your hearts. For as members
of one body you are called to live
in peace. And always be thankful.

Colossians 3:15 NLT

To set the mind on the
Spirit is life and peace.

Romans 8:6 ESV

The kingdom of God is not a matter
of eating and drinking but of righteousness
and peace and joy in the Holy Spirit.
Whoever thus serves Christ is acceptable
to God and approved by men. So then
let us pursue what makes for peace
and for mutual upbuilding.

Romans 14:17-19 ESV

PURPOSE

"For this purpose I have raised you up,
to show you My power, so that My name
may be proclaimed in all the earth."

Exodus 9:16 ESV

We know that in all things God works for
the good of those who love Him, who have
been called according to His purpose.

Romans 8:28 NIV

Purpose

Rejoice always, pray without ceasing,
give thanks in all circumstances; for this
is the will of God in Christ Jesus for you.

1 Thessalonians 5:16-18 ESV

I am sure of this, that He who began
a good work in you will bring it to
completion at the day of Jesus Christ.

Philippians 1:6 ESV

Teach me to do Your will, for You are
my God. May Your gracious Spirit
lead me forward on a firm footing.

Psalm 143:10 NLT

Purpose

The LORD will fulfill His purpose for me;
Your steadfast love, O LORD, endures forever.

Psalm 138:8 ESV

Whether you turn to the right or to the left,
your ears will hear a voice behind you,
saying, "This is the way; walk in it."

Isaiah 30:21 NIV

Everything else is worthless when compared
with the infinite value of knowing
Christ Jesus my Lord. For His sake I have
discarded everything else, counting
it all as garbage, so that I could gain
Christ and become one with Him.

Philippians 3:8-9 NLT

Purpose

I cry out to God Most High, to God
who fulfills His purpose for me.

Psalm 57:2 ESV

Many are the plans in a person's heart,
but it is the LORD's purpose that prevails.

Proverbs 19:21 NIV

"You are the light of the world. A city set
on a hill cannot be hidden. Nor do people
light a lamp and put it under a basket,
but on a stand, and it gives light to all in
the house. In the same way, let your light
shine before others, so that they may
see your good works and give glory
to your Father who is in heaven."

Matthew 5:14-16 ESV

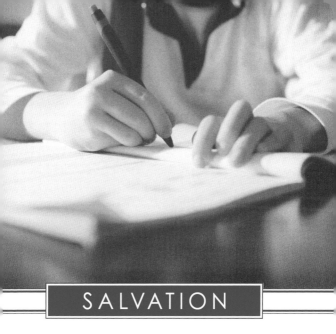

SALVATION

There is salvation in no one else!
God has given no other name under
heaven by which we must be saved.

Acts 4:12 NLT

For God so loved the world, that He gave
His only Son, that whoever believes in Him
should not perish but have eternal life.

John 3:16 ESV

God shows His love for us in that while we were still sinners, Christ died for us.

Romans 5:8 ESV

"Though your sins are like scarlet, they shall be as white as snow; though they are red as crimson, they shall be like wool."

Isaiah 1:18 NIV

All have sinned and fall short of the glory of God, and all are justified freely by His grace through the redemption that came by Christ Jesus.

Romans 3:23-24 NIV

Salvation

God saved you by His grace when you
believed. And you can't take credit for this;
it is a gift from God. Salvation is not a reward
for the good things we have done,
so none of us can boast about it.

Ephesians 2:8-9 NLT

The wages of sin is death, but the gift of
God is eternal life in Christ Jesus our Lord.

Romans 6:23 NIV

"Here I am! I stand at the door and knock.
If anyone hears My voice and opens the
door, I will come in and eat with
that person, and they with Me."

Revelation 3:20 NIV

Salvation

Repent of your sins and turn to God, so that your sins may be wiped away. Then times of refreshment will come from the presence of the Lord, and He will again send you Jesus, your appointed Messiah.

Acts 3:19-20 NLT

"Everyone who acknowledges Me before men, I also will acknowledge before My Father who is in heaven."

Matthew 10:32 ESV

STRENGTH

"My grace is all you need.
My power works best in weakness."

2 Corinthians 12:9 NLT

I can do everything through Christ,
who gives me strength.

Philippians 4:13 NLT

Strength

The LORD is my strength and my song;
He has given me victory.
This is my God, and I will praise Him.

Exodus 15:2 NLT

It is God who arms me with
strength and keeps my way secure.
He makes my feet like the feet of a deer;
He causes me to stand on the heights.

2 Samuel 22:33-34 NIV

My flesh and my heart may fail,
but God is the strength of my
heart and my portion forever.

Psalm 73:26 ESV

Strength

He gives power to the weak and
strength to the powerless.

Isaiah 40:29 NLT

You have armed me with
strength for the battle; You have
subdued my enemies under my feet.

2 Samuel 22:40 NLT

The LORD gives strength to His people;
the LORD blesses His people with peace.

Psalm 29:11 NIV

Strength

The Sovereign LORD is my strength!
He makes me as surefooted as a deer,
able to tread upon the heights.

Habakkuk 3:19 NLT

Be strong in the Lord and
in His mighty power.

Ephesians 6:10 NLT

The joy of the LORD is your strength!

Nehemiah 8:10 NLT

SUCCESS

The Lord, before whom I have walked
faithfully, will send His angel with you
and make your journey a success.

Genesis 24:40 NIV

Not that we are sufficient in ourselves
to claim anything as coming from us,
but our sufficiency is from God.

2 Corinthians 3:5 ESV

Success

The reward for humility and fear of the Lord is riches and honor and life.

Proverbs 22:4 ESV

May God grant your heart's desires and make all your plans succeed.

Psalm 20:4 NLT

My cup overflows with blessings. Surely Your goodness and unfailing love will pursue me all the days of my life, and I will live in the house of the Lord forever.

Psalm 23:5-6 NLT

Success

Commit your actions to the Lord,
and your plans will succeed.

Proverbs 16:3 NLT

Whoever brings blessing will be
enriched, and one who waters
will himself be watered.

Proverbs 11:25 ESV

The Lord will make you the head and not
the tail, and you shall only go up and not
down, if you obey the commandments of
the Lord your God, which I command
you today, being careful to do them.

Deuteronomy 28:13 ESV

Success

Commit everything you do to the LORD.
Trust Him, and He will help you.

Psalm 37:5 NLT

With God's help we will do mighty things.

Psalm 60:12 NLT

"I know the plans I have for you," says the
LORD. "They are plans for good and not for
disaster, to give you a future and a hope."

Jeremiah 29:11 NLT

WISDOM

The Lord gives wisdom; from His mouth
come knowledge and understanding.

Proverbs 2:6 NIV

To one person the Spirit gives the ability to
give wise advice; to another the same Spirit
gives a message of special knowledge.

1 Corinthians 12:8 NLT

Wisdom

Fear of the Lord is the foundation of true
wisdom. All who obey His commandments
will grow in wisdom. Praise Him forever!

Psalm 111:10 NLT

The wise are mightier than the strong,
and those with knowledge grow
stronger and stronger.

Proverbs 24:5 NLT

If any of you lacks wisdom, you should ask
God, who gives generously to all without
finding fault, and it will be given to you.

James 1:5 NIV

Wisdom

Wise words satisfy like a good meal;
the right words bring satisfaction.

Proverbs 18:20 NLT

In the same way, wisdom is
sweet to your soul. If you find it,
you will have a bright future,
and your hopes will not be cut short.

Proverbs 24:14 NLT

You're blessed when you meet Lady Wisdom,
when you make friends with Madame Insight.
She's worth far more than money in the bank;
her friendship is better than a big salary.
Her value exceeds all the trappings
of wealth; nothing you could wish
for holds a candle to her.

Proverbs 3:13-15 MSG

Wisdom

Tune your ears to the world of Wisdom;
set your heart on a life of Understanding.
That's right, if you make Insight your priority,
and won't take no for an answer,
searching for it like a prospector panning
for gold, like an adventurer on a treasure
hunt, believe me, before you know it
Fear-of-God will be yours; you'll have
come upon the Knowledge of God.

Proverbs 2:2-5 MSG

Wisdom will enter your heart,
and knowledge will fill you with joy.
Wise choices will watch over you.
Understanding will keep you safe.

Proverbs 2:10-11 NLT

WHEN THE GRADUATE NEEDS ...

COMFORT

God is our merciful Father and the source of
all comfort. He comforts us in all our troubles
so that we can comfort others. When
they are troubled, we will be able to give
them the same comfort God has given us.

2 Corinthians 1:3-4 NLT

Do not be afraid or discouraged,
for the LORD will personally go
ahead of you. He will be with you;
He will neither fail you nor abandon you.

Deuteronomy 31:8 NLT

Comfort

Lord, You know the hopes of the
helpless. Surely You will hear
their cries and comfort them.

Psalm 10:17 NLT

Yet I still belong to You;
You hold my right hand.

Psalm 73:23 NLT

"As a mother comforts her child,
so will I comfort you."

Isaiah 66:13 NIV

Comfort

"Do not be afraid, for I am
with you and will bless you."

Genesis 26:24 NLT

You, O Lord, help and comfort me.

Psalm 86:17 NLT

Pile your troubles on God's shoulders –
He'll carry your load, He'll help you out.
He'll never let good people topple into ruin.
But You, God, will throw the others into a
muddy bog, cut the lifespan of assassins
and traitors in half. And I trust You.

Psalm 55:22-23 MSG

Comfort

"Come to Me, all of you who are
weary and carry heavy burdens,
and I will give you rest."

Matthew 11:28 NLT

Cast all your anxiety on Him
because He cares for you.

1 Peter 5:7 NIV

"When you pass through the waters, I will be
with you; and when you pass through the
rivers, they will not sweep over you. When
you walk through the fire, you will not be
burned. For I am the LORD your God."

Isaiah 43:2-3 NIV

CONFIDENCE

The Lord will be your confidence and will keep your foot from being caught.

Proverbs 3:26 ESV

I have confidence from the Lord.

Philippians 2:24 NLT

Confidence

We have confidence before God and
receive from Him anything we ask.

1 John 3:21-22 NIV

Whatever I have, wherever I am,
I can make it through anything in
the One who makes me who I am.

Philippians 4:13 MSG

You have been my hope, Sovereign LORD,
my confidence since my youth.

Psalm 71:5 NIV

Confidence

Blessed are those who trust in
the Lord and have made the
Lord their hope and confidence.

Jeremiah 17:7 NLT

So we can confidently say,
"The Lord is my helper; I will not fear;
what can man do to me?"

Hebrews 13:6 ESV

God doesn't want us to be shy with His
gifts, but bold and loving and sensible.

2 Timothy 1:7 MSG

Confidence

I know the LORD is always with me. I will
not be shaken, for He is right beside me.

Psalm 16:8 NLT

Be strong and do not give up,
for your work will be rewarded.

2 Chronicles 15:7 NIV

The eternal God is your refuge, and
underneath are the everlasting arms.

Deuteronomy 33:27 NIV

COURAGE

Be strong and courageous! Do not be afraid
or discouraged. For the LORD your God
is with you wherever you go.

Joshua 1:9 NLT

Be on guard. Stand firm in the faith.
Be courageous. Be strong.

1 Corinthians 16:13 NLT

Courage

Wait for the Lord; be strong, and let your heart take courage; wait for the Lord!

Psalm 27:14 ESV

"Don't panic. I'm with you. There's no need to fear for I'm your God. I'll give you strength. I'll help you. I'll hold you steady, keep a firm grip on you."

Isaiah 41:10 MSG

Even when I walk through the darkest valley, I will not be afraid, for You are close beside me. Your rod and Your staff protect and comfort me.

Psalm 23:4 NLT

Courage

I sought the Lord, and He answered me
and delivered me from all my fears.

Psalm 34:4 ESV

The Lord is my light and my salvation –
so why should I be afraid? The Lord is my
fortress, protecting me from danger,
so why should I tremble?

Psalm 27:1 NLT

He will order His angels to protect you
wherever you go. They will hold you
up with their hands so you won't
even hurt your foot on a stone.

Psalm 91:11-12 NLT

Courage

With my God I can scale any wall.

Psalm 18:29 NLT

Be strong and courageous, all you
who put your hope in the Lord!

Psalm 31:24 NLT

"Though the mountains be shaken and the
hills be removed, yet My unfailing love for
you will not be shaken nor My covenant
of peace be removed," says the Lord,
who has compassion on you.

Isaiah 54:10 NIV

ENCOURAGEMENT

May our Lord Jesus Christ Himself and God
our Father, who loved us and by His grace
gave us eternal encouragement and good
hope, encourage your hearts and strengthen
you in every good deed and word.

2 Thessalonians 2:16-17 NIV

Stay with God! Take heart. Don't quit.
I'll say it again: Stay with God.

Psalm 27:14 MSG

Encouragement

"Do not worry about your life, what you
will eat or drink; or about your body,
what you will wear. Is not life more than food,
and the body more than clothes?
Look at the birds of the air; they do not
sow or reap or store away in barns, and
yet your heavenly Father feeds them.
Are you not much more valuable than they?"

Matthew 6:25-26 NIV

Let all who seek God's help be encouraged.

Psalm 69:32 NLT

The Lord your God is in your midst,
a mighty One who will save;
He will rejoice over you with gladness;
He will quiet you by His love; He will exult
over you with loud singing.

Zephaniah 3:17 ESV

Such things were written in the Scriptures
long ago to teach us. And the Scriptures give
us hope and encouragement as we wait
patiently for God's promises to be fulfilled.

Romans 15:4 NLT

Humble yourselves before the Lord,
and He will lift you up.

James 4:10 NIV

Don't worry about anything; instead,
pray about everything. Tell God what you
need, and thank Him for all He has done.
Then you will experience God's peace,
which exceeds anything we can understand.
His peace will guard your hearts and
minds as you live in Christ Jesus.

Philippians 4:6-7 NLT

The LORD your God fights for
you, just as He promised.

Joshua 23:10 NLT

Blessed be the God and Father of
our Lord Jesus Christ, who has blessed
us in Christ with every spiritual
blessing in the heavenly places.

Ephesians 1:3 ESV

"The grass withers and the flowers fall, but
the word of our God endures forever."

Isaiah 40:8 NIV

GUIDANCE

The LORD says, "I will guide you
along the best pathway for your life.
I will advise you and watch over you."

Psalm 32:8 NLT

God is our God for ever and ever;
He will be our guide even to the end.

Psalm 48:14 NIV

Guidance

God, teach me lessons for living so
I can stay the course. Give me insight
so I can do what You tell me.

Psalm 119:33-34 MSG

I will bless the LORD who guides me;
even at night my heart instructs me.

Psalm 16:7 NLT

The LORD Himself goes before you
and will be with you; He will never
leave you nor forsake you. Do not
be afraid; do not be discouraged.

Deuteronomy 31:8 NIV

Guidance

I look up to the mountains; does my strength
come from mountains? No, my strength
comes from God, who made heaven,
and earth, and mountains.

Psalm 121:1-2 MSG

The LORD will guide you always.

Isaiah 58:11 NIV

"When the Spirit of truth comes, He will
guide you into all truth. He will not speak on
His own but will tell you what He has heard.
He will tell you about the future."

John 16:13 NLT

Guidance

Show me how You work, God; school me in
Your ways. Take me by the hand; lead me
down the path of truth. You are my Savior.

Psalm 25:4-5 MSG

Your word is a lamp to guide
my feet and a light for my path.

Psalm 119:105 NLT

Be imitators of God, as beloved children.
And walk in love, as Christ loved us
and gave Himself up for us, a fragrant
offering and sacrifice to God.

Ephesians 5:1-2 ESV

HOPE

There is one body and one Spirit,
just as you have been called to
one glorious hope for the future.

Ephesians 4:4 NLT

The Lord delights in those who fear Him,
who put their hope in His unfailing love.

Psalm 147:11 NIV

Hope

The LORD is good to those
whose hope is in Him.

Lamentations 3:25 NIV

God can pour on the blessings in astonishing
ways so that you're ready for anything
and everything, more than just ready
to do what needs to be done.

2 Corinthians 9:8 MSG

Why am I discouraged? Why is my heart so
sad? I will put my hope in God! I will praise
Him again – my Savior and my God!

Psalm 42:5-6 NLT

Hope

Rejoice in hope, be patient in tribulation,
be constant in prayer.

Romans 12:12 ESV

May integrity and honesty protect me,
for I put my hope in You.

Psalm 25:21 NLT

May the God of hope fill you
with all joy and peace as you trust
in Him, so that you may overflow with
hope by the power of the Holy Spirit.

Romans 15:13 NIV

Hope

Blessed be the God and Father of
our Lord Jesus Christ! According to
His great mercy, He has caused us to be
born again to a living hope through
the resurrection of Jesus Christ.

1 Peter 1:3 ESV

Blessed are those whose help is the
God of Jacob, whose hope is in the LORD
their God. He is the Maker of heaven
and earth, the sea, and everything in
them – He remains faithful forever.

Psalm 146:5-6 NIV

I wait for the LORD, my whole being
waits, and in His word I put my hope.

Psalm 130:5 NIV

LOVE

Give thanks to the LORD, for He is good!
His faithful love endures forever.

Psalm 118:29 NLT

Everything God does is right –
the trademark on all His works is love.

Psalm 145:17 MSG

Love

This is the kind of love we are talking about – not that we once upon a time loved God, but that He loved us and sent His Son as a sacrifice to clear away our sins and the damage they've done to our relationship with God.

1 John 4:10 MSG

I am convinced that nothing can ever separate us from God's love. Neither death nor life, neither angels nor demons, neither our fears for today nor our worries about tomorrow – not even the powers of hell can separate us from God's love.

Romans 8:38 NLT

"There is no greater love than to lay down one's life for one's friends."

John 15:13 NLT

Love

God shows His love for us in that while we
were still sinners, Christ died for us.

Romans 5:8 ESV

This is how much God loved the world:
He gave His Son, His one and only Son.
And this is why: so that no one need
be destroyed; by believing in Him,
anyone can have a whole and lasting life.

John 3:16 MSG

God is so rich in mercy, and He loved us
so much, that even though we were dead
because of our sins, He gave us life when
He raised Christ from the dead.

Ephesians 2:4-5 NLT

Love each other deeply
with all your heart.

1 Peter 1:22 NLT

Love will last forever.

1 Corinthians 13:8 NLT

God is love. Whoever lives in love lives
in God, and God in them. This is how
love is made complete among us.

1 John 4:16-17 NIV

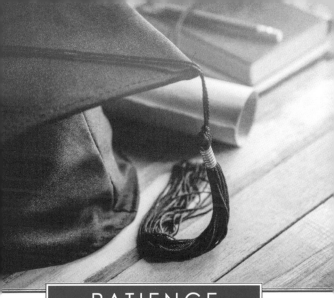

PATIENCE

I waited patiently for the Lord to help me,
and He turned to me and heard my cry.

Psalm 40:1 NLT

If we look forward to something
we don't yet have, we must wait
patiently and confidently.

Romans 8:25 NLT

Patience

The Lord isn't really being slow about
His promise, as some people think.
No, He is being patient for your sake.
He does not want anyone to be destroyed,
but wants everyone to repent.

2 Peter 3:9 NLT

Let's keep a firm grip on the promises that
keep us going. He always keeps His word.

Hebrews 10:23 MSG

Quiet down before God,
be prayerful before Him.
Don't bother with those
who climb the ladder,
who elbow their way to the top.

Psalm 37:7 MSG

Patience

The LORD is good to those who wait
for Him, to the soul who seeks Him.
It is good that one should wait quietly for
the salvation of the LORD. It is good for
a man that he bear the yoke in his youth.

Lamentations 3:25-27 ESV

May God, who gives this patience and
encouragement, help you live in complete
harmony with each other, as is fitting for
followers of Christ Jesus. Then all of you
can join together with one voice, giving
praise and glory to God, the Father
of our Lord Jesus Christ.

Romans 15:5-6 NLT

You, O LORD, are a God of compassion and
mercy, slow to get angry and filled with
unfailing love and faithfulness.

Psalm 86:15 NLT

Patience

Chosen by God for this new life of love,
dress in the wardrobe God picked out for
you: compassion, kindness, humility,
quiet strength, discipline.

Colossians 3:12 MSG

Always be humble and gentle. Be patient
with each other, making allowance for
each other's faults because of your love.

Ephesians 4:2 NLT

It is good to wait quietly for
the salvation of the LORD.

Lamentations 3:26 NIV

PERSEVERANCE

You need to persevere so that when
you have done the will of God, you will
receive what He has promised.

Hebrews 10:36 NIV

Let perseverance finish its work so
that you may be mature and complete,
not lacking anything.

James 1:4 NIV

Perseverance

Blessed is the one who perseveres under trial because, having stood the test, that person will receive the crown of life that the Lord has promised to those who love Him.

James 1:12 NIV

Since we are surrounded by such a great cloud of witnesses, let us throw off everything that hinders and the sin that so easily entangles. And let us run with perseverance the race marked out for us.

Hebrews 12:1 NIV

Always be humble and gentle. Be patient with each other, making allowance for each other's faults because of your love.

Ephesians 4:2 NLT

Perseverance

The end of a matter is better than its
beginning, and patience is better than pride.

Ecclesiastes 7:8 NIV

Consider it a sheer gift, friends,
when tests and challenges come at you
from all sides. You know that under pressure,
your faith-life is forced into the open and
shows its true colors. So don't try to get
out of anything prematurely. Let it do
its work so you become mature and
well-developed, not deficient in any way.

James 1:2-4 MSG

My life is worth nothing to me
unless I use it for finishing the work
assigned me by the Lord Jesus – the work
of telling others the Good News
about the wonderful grace of God.

Acts 20:24 NLT

Perseverance

The LORD is my rock and my fortress
and my deliverer, my God, my rock,
in whom I take refuge, my shield, and
the horn of my salvation, my stronghold.

Psalm 18:2 ESV

"Since you have kept My command
to endure patiently, I will also keep you
from the hour of trial that is going
to come on the whole world to
test the inhabitants of the earth."

Revelation 3:10 NIV

Be strong and do not give up,
for your work will be rewarded.

2 Chronicles 15:7 NIV

PROTECTION

Even though I walk through
the valley of the shadow of death,
I will fear no evil, for You are with me;
Your rod and Your staff, they comfort me.

Psalm 23:4 ESV

Guard me as You would guard Your own eyes.
Hide me in the shadow of Your wings.

Psalm 17:8 NLT

Protection

My God is my rock, in whom I find
protection. He is my shield, the
power that saves me, and my place
of safety. He is my refuge, my Savior,
the one who saves me from violence.

2 Samuel 22:3 NLT

God's a safe-house for the battered,
a sanctuary during bad times.
The moment you arrive, you relax;
you're never sorry you knocked.

Psalm 9:9 MSG

The LORD Himself goes before you and
will be with you; He will never leave you
nor forsake you. Do not be afraid.

Deuteronomy 31:8 NIV

Protection

The LORD says, "I will rescue those
who love Me. I will protect
those who trust in My name."

Psalm 91:14 NLT

God's angel sets up a circle of
protection around us while we pray.
Open your mouth and taste, open
your eyes and see – how good God is.
Blessed are you who run to Him.

Psalm 34:7-8 MSG

If you make the LORD your refuge, if
you make the Most High your shelter,
no evil will conquer you; no plague will
come near your home. For He will order
His angels to protect you wherever you go.

Psalm 91:9-11 NLT

Protection

God guards you from every evil, He guards
your very life. He guards you when you
leave and when you return, He guards
you now, He guards you always.

Psalm 121:7-8 MSG

God's name is a place of protection –
good people can run there and be safe.

Proverbs 18:10 MSG

In peace I will lie down and sleep, for You
alone, LORD, make me dwell in safety.

Psalm 4:8 NIV

REST

My heart is glad, and I rejoice.
My body rests in safety.

Psalm 16:9 NLT

"Come to Me, all of you who are
weary and carry heavy burdens,
and I will give you rest."

Matthew 11:28 NLT

Rest

God has told His people, "Here is
a place of rest; let the weary rest here.
This is a place of quiet rest."

Isaiah 28:12 NLT

Blessed is the man who trusts in the LORD,
whose trust is the LORD. He is like a tree
planted by water, that sends out its roots by
the stream, and does not fear when heat
comes, for its leaves remain green, and
is not anxious in the year of drought, for it
does not cease to bear fruit.

Jeremiah 17:7-8 ESV

This is what the Sovereign LORD, the Holy One
of Israel, says: "Only in returning to
Me and resting in Me will you be saved.
In quietness and confidence is your strength."

Isaiah 30:15 NLT

Rest

God said, "My presence will go with you.
I'll see the journey to the end."

Exodus 33:14 MSG

I wait quietly before God, for my
victory comes from Him. He alone is
my rock and my salvation, my fortress
where I will never be shaken.

Psalm 62:1-2 NLT

Whoever dwells in the shelter of the Most
High will rest in the shadow of the Almighty. I
will say of the LORD, "He is my refuge and my
fortress, my God, in whom I trust."

Psalm 91:1-2 NIV

Rest

He makes me lie down in green pastures,
He leads me beside quiet waters,
He refreshes my soul. He guides me
along the right paths for His name's sake.

Psalm 23:2-3 NIV

Whoever has entered God's rest has also
rested from his works as God did from His.

Hebrews 4:10 ESV

You will restore my life again;
from the depths of the earth
You will again bring me up.

Psalm 71:20 NIV

Words of wisdom for the graduate on ...

AMBITION

Make it your ambition to lead a quiet life:
You should mind your own business and work with
your hands, just as we told you, so that your daily
life may win the respect of outsiders and so that
you will not be dependent on anybody.

1 Thessalonians 4:11-12 NIV

"Seek the Kingdom of God above all
else, and live righteously, and He will
give you everything you need."

Matthew 6:33 NLT

Ambition

All that is in the world – the desires
of the flesh and the desires of the eyes
and pride in possessions – is not from
the Father but is from the world.

1 John 2:16 ESV

Now all glory to God, who is able,
through His mighty power at work
within us, to accomplish infinitely
more than we might ask or think.

Ephesians 3:20 NLT

I discipline my body like an athlete,
training it to do what it should.
Otherwise, I fear that after preaching to
others I myself might be disqualified.

1 Corinthians 9:27 NLT

Ambition

Brothers, I do not consider that I have
made it my own. But one thing I do:
forgetting what lies behind and straining
forward to what lies ahead, I press on
toward the goal for the prize of
the upward call of God in Christ Jesus.

Philippians 3:13-14 ESV

My ambition has always been to
preach the Good News where the
name of Christ has never been heard.

Romans 15:20 NLT

Joyful are people of integrity,
who follow the instructions of the LORD.
Joyful are those who obey His laws and
search for Him with all their hearts.

Psalm 119:1-2 NLT

Ambition

Strive to excel in building up the church.

1 Corinthians 14:12 ESV

Strive for peace with everyone,
and for the holiness without
which no one will see the Lord.

Hebrews 12:14 ESV

The desire of the righteous
ends only in good.

Proverbs 11:23 NIV

CHARACTER

Endurance develops strength of
character, and character strengthens
our confident hope of salvation.

Romans 5:4 NLT

"God blesses those whose hearts
are pure, for they will see God."

Matthew 5:8 NLT

Character

May you always be filled with the fruit of
your salvation – the righteous character
produced in your life by Jesus Christ – for this
will bring much glory and praise to God.

Philippians 1:11 NLT

A good name is more desirable
than great riches; to be esteemed
is better than silver or gold.

Proverbs 22:1 NIV

Judge nothing before the appointed time;
wait until the Lord comes. He will bring to
light what is hidden in darkness and will
expose the motives of the heart. At that
time each will receive their praise from God.

1 Corinthians 4:5 NIV

Character

The LORD God is our sun and our
shield. He gives us grace and glory.
The LORD will withhold no good
thing from those who do what is right.

Psalm 84:11 NLT

How can a young person stay pure?
By obeying Your word.

Psalm 119:9 NLT

The fruit of the Spirit is love, joy,
peace, patience, kindness, goodness,
faithfulness, gentleness, self-control;
against such things there is no law.

Galatians 5:22-23 ESV

Character

There will be glory and honor and
peace from God for all who do good.

Romans 2:10 NLT

God is working in you, giving you the desire
and power to do what pleases Him.

Philippians 2:13 NLT

Live a life filled with love, following
the example of Christ. He loved us
and offered Himself as a sacrifice
for us, a pleasing aroma to God.

Ephesians 5:2 NLT

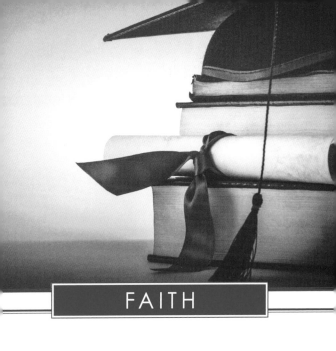

FAITH

If you do not stand firm in your faith,
you will not stand at all.

Isaiah 7:9 NIV

Fight the good fight for the true faith.
Hold tightly to the eternal life to
which God has called you.

1 Timothy 6:12 NLT

"Anything is possible if a person believes."

Mark 9:23 NLT

The fundamental fact of existence is
that this trust in God, this faith, is the
firm foundation under everything that
makes life worth living. It's our
handle on what we can't see.

Hebrews 11:1 MSG

"If you have faith as small as a mustard
seed, you can say to this mulberry tree,
'Be uprooted and planted in the sea,'
and it will obey you."

Luke 17:6 NIV

By grace you have been saved through
faith. And this is not your own doing;
it is the gift of God, not a result of works,
so that no one may boast.

Ephesians 2:8-9 ESV

Just as you accepted Christ Jesus as your
Lord, you must continue to follow Him. Let
your roots grow down into Him, and let your
lives be built on Him. Then your faith will
grow strong in the truth you were taught,
and you will overflow with thankfulness.

Colossians 2:6-7 NLT

"I tell you the truth, those who listen
to My message and believe in God
who sent Me have eternal life."

John 5:24 NLT

Faith

We fix our eyes not on what is seen,
but on what is unseen, since what is seen
is temporary, but what is unseen is eternal.

2 Corinthians 4:18 NIV

We walk by faith, not by sight.

2 Corinthians 5:7 ESV

"Before I formed you in the womb I knew
you, before you were born I set you apart."

Jeremiah 1:5 NIV

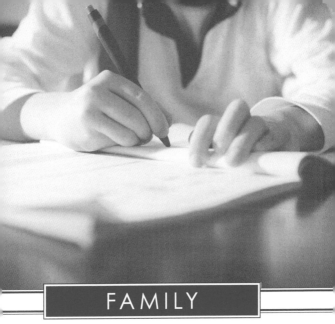

FAMILY

"I will be your Father, and you will be My sons and daughters," says the Lord Almighty.

2 Corinthians 6:18 NLT

You are members of God's family.

Ephesians 2:19 NLT

Family

If anyone does not know how to
manage his own family, how
can he take care of God's church?

1 Timothy 3:5 NIV

God decided in advance to adopt us into
His own family by bringing us to Himself
through Jesus Christ. This is what He wanted
to do, and it gave Him great pleasure.

Ephesians 1:5 NLT

What marvelous love the Father has
extended to us! Just look at it – we're called
children of God! That's who we really
are. But that's also why the world doesn't
recognize us or take us seriously, because it
has no idea who He is or what He's up to.

1 John 3:1 MSG

Family

Of His own will He brought us forth by the
word of truth, that we should be a kind of
firstfruits of His creatures.

James 1:18 ESV

My son, obey your father's commands,
and don't neglect your mother's instruction.
Keep their words always in your heart.
Tie them around your neck.

Proverbs 6:20-21 NLT

As for me and my family,
we'll worship God.

Joshua 24:15 MSG

Family

Honor your father and your mother,
that your days may be long.

Exodus 20:12 ESV

Jesus said, "The person who obeys God's
will is My brother and sister and mother."

Mark 3:35 MSG

Jesus and the ones He makes
holy have the same Father.
That is why Jesus is not ashamed
to call them His brothers and sisters.

Hebrews 2:11 NLT

FRIENDSHIP

Friends love through all kinds of
weather, and families stick
together in all kinds of trouble.

Proverbs 17:17 MSG

Friends come and friends go,
but a true friend sticks by you like family.

Proverbs 18:24 MSG

Friendship

As iron sharpens iron,
so a friend sharpens a friend.

Proverbs 27:17 NLT

Two people are better off than one,
for they can help each other succeed.

Ecclesiastes 4:9 NLT

Now we can rejoice in our wonderful new
relationship with God because our Lord
Jesus Christ has made us friends of God.

Romans 5:11 NLT

How good and pleasant it is when God's
people live together in unity!

Psalm 133:1 NIV

If we walk in the light, as He is in the
light, we have fellowship with one
another, and the blood of Jesus
His Son cleanses us from all sin.

1 John 1:7 ESV

"Where two or three gather in
My name, there I am with them."

Matthew 18:20 NIV

Friendship

The heartfelt counsel of a friend
is as sweet as perfume and incense.

Proverbs 27:9 NLT

Bear one another's burdens,
and so fulfill the law of Christ.

Galatians 6:2 ESV

"Love each other in the same way I have
loved you. There is no greater love than to
lay down one's life for one's friends."

John 15:12-13 NLT

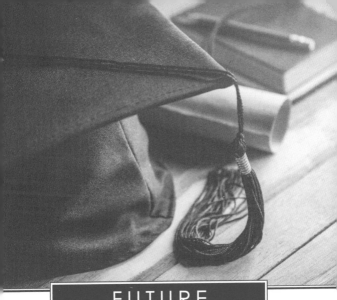

FUTURE

"I know the plans I have for you,"
declares the LORD, "plans to prosper
you and not to harm you, plans
to give you hope and a future."

Jeremiah 29:11 NIV

There is surely a future hope for you,
and your hope will not be cut off.

Proverbs 23:18 NIV

Your beginnings will seem humble,
so prosperous will your future be.

Job 8:7 NIV

The LORD will fulfill His purpose for me;
Your steadfast love, O LORD, endures forever.
Do not forsake the work of Your hands.

Psalm 138:8 ESV

The LORD leads with unfailing
love and faithfulness all who keep His
covenant and obey His demands.

Psalm 25:10 NLT

Future

Teach me to do Your will,
for You are my God! Let Your good
Spirit lead me on level ground.

Psalm 143:10 ESV

"Do not let your hearts be troubled.
You believe in God; believe also in Me."

John 14:1 NIV

Wisdom is like honey for you: If you
find it, there is a future hope for you,
and your hope will not be cut off.

Proverbs 24:14 NIV

The Lord will reign forever and ever.

Revelation 11:15 NLT

Jesus said: "Soon you'll see it for yourself:
The Son of Man seated at the
right hand of the Mighty One,
arriving on the clouds of heaven."

Matthew 26:64 MSG

Grow in the grace and knowledge of our
Lord and Savior Jesus Christ. To Him be the
glory both now and to the day of eternity.

2 Peter 3:18 ESV

GOALS

Cheerfully pleasing God is the main
thing, and that's what we aim to do.

2 Corinthians 5:9 MSG

What I am commanding you today is not
too difficult for you or beyond your reach.

Deuteronomy 30:11 NIV

Goals

Now listen, you who say, "Today or tomorrow we will go to this or that city, spend a year there, carry on business and make money." Why, you do not even know what will happen tomorrow. What is your life? You are a mist that appears for a little while and then vanishes. Instead, you ought to say, "If it is the Lord's will, we will live and do this or that." As it is, you boast in your arrogant schemes. All such boasting is evil.

James 4:13-16 NIV

Do not conform to the pattern of this world, but be transformed by the renewing of your mind. Then you will be able to test and approve what God's will is – His good, pleasing and perfect will.

Romans 12:2 NIV

Goals

When God approves of your life,
even your enemies will end up shaking
your hand. Far better to be right and
poor than to be wrong and rich.

Proverbs 16:7-8 MSG

I press on to possess that perfection for
which Christ Jesus first possessed me.
I focus on this one thing: Forgetting the past
and looking forward to what lies ahead,
I press on to reach the end of the race and
receive the heavenly prize for which God,
through Christ Jesus, is calling us.

Philippians 3:12-14 NLT

Let's not allow ourselves to get fatigued
doing good. At the right time we will harvest
a good crop if we don't give up, or quit.

Galatians 6:9 MSG

Goals

It is pleasant to see dreams come true.

Proverbs 13:19 NLT

"Where your treasure is,
there your heart will be also."

Matthew 6:21 NIV

May He give you the desire of your heart
and make all your plans succeed.

Psalm 20:4 NIV

"I am the LORD your God,
who teaches you to profit, who leads
you in the way you should go."

Isaiah 48:17 ESV

GRATITUDE

Let us be thankful and please
God by worshiping Him.

Hebrews 12:28 NLT

Be thankful in all circumstances,
for this is God's will for you who
belong to Christ Jesus.

1 Thessalonians 5:18 NLT

Gratitude

Since everything God created is
good, we should not reject any
of it but receive it with thanks.

1 Timothy 4:4 NLT

Thank God! Call out His Name!
Tell the whole world who He is and
what He's done! Sing to Him! Play songs
for Him! Broadcast all His wonders!

1 Chronicles 16:8-9 MSG

May you be filled with joy,
always thanking the Father. He has enabled
you to share in the inheritance that belongs
to His people, who live in the light.

Colossians 1:11-12 NLT

Gratitude

Thanks be to God, who gives us the
victory through our Lord Jesus Christ.

1 Corinthians 15:57 ESV

Thanks be to God, who in Christ always
leads us in triumphal procession,
and through us spreads the fragrance
of the knowledge of Him everywhere.

2 Corinthians 2:14 ESV

Give thanks to the LORD, for He is good!
His faithful love endures forever.

1 Chronicles 16:34 NLT

Gratitude

Praise the Lord! I will give thanks to the Lord
with my whole heart, in the company
of the upright, in the congregation.
Great are the works of the Lord,
studied by all who delight in them.

Psalm 111:1-2 ESV

The Lord has done great things for us,
and we are filled with joy.

Psalm 126:3 NIV

We thank You, O God! We give
thanks because You are near. People
everywhere tell of Your wonderful deeds.

Psalm 75:1 NLT

HUMILITY

Humble yourselves under the
mighty power of God, and at the
right time He will lift you up in honor.

1 Peter 5:6 NLT

Don't be selfish; don't try to impress others.
Be humble, thinking of others
as better than yourselves.

Philippians 2:3 NLT

Humility

Humble yourselves before the Lord,
and He will lift you up in honor.

James 4:10 NLT

Those who exalt themselves will
be humbled, and those who humble
themselves will be exalted.

Luke 14:11 NLT

"Whoever would be great among you must
be your servant, and whoever would be
first among you must be your slave."

Matthew 20:26-27 ESV

Humility

Don't think you are better than you
really are. Be honest in your evaluation
of yourselves, measuring yourselves
by the faith God has given us.

Romans 12:3 NLT

God opposes the proud,
but gives grace to the humble.

James 4:6 ESV

When pride comes, then comes disgrace,
but with the humble is wisdom.

Proverbs 11:2 ESV

Humility

He leads the humble in what is right,
and teaches the humble His way.

Psalm 25:9 ESV

Pride lands you flat on your face;
humility prepares you for honors.

Proverbs 29:23 MSG

"Anyone who becomes as humble
as this little child is the greatest
in the Kingdom of Heaven."

Matthew 18:4 NLT

PRAYER

The earnest prayer of a righteous person has
great power and produces wonderful results.

James 5:16 NLT

"Ask and it will be given to you; seek and you
will find; knock and the door will be opened to
you. For everyone who asks receives;
the one who seeks finds; and to the one
who knocks, the door will be opened."

Matthew 7:7-8 NIV

Prayer

Never stop praying.

1 Thessalonians 5:17 NLT

Don't fret or worry. Instead of
worrying, pray. Let petitions and
praises shape your worries into prayers,
letting God know your concerns.

Philippians 4:6 MSG

God's there, listening for all who pray,
for all who pray and mean it.

Psalm 145:18 MSG

Prayer

Don't quit in hard times; pray all the harder.

Romans 12:12 MSG

This is what the LORD says, He who
made the earth, the LORD who formed it
and established it – the LORD is His name:
"Call to Me and I will answer you
and tell you great and unsearchable
things you do not know."

Jeremiah 33:2-3 NIV

Let us then with confidence draw near to the
throne of grace, that we may receive mercy
and find grace to help in time of need.

Hebrews 4:16 ESV

Prayer

"When you pray, go away by yourself, shut
the door behind you, and pray to your
Father in private. Then your Father,
who sees everything, will reward you."

Matthew 6:6 NLT

"I will answer them before they even
call to Me. While they are still talking
about their needs, I will go ahead
and answer their prayers!"

Isaiah 65:24 NLT

You must build each other up
in your most holy faith, pray in
the power of the Holy Spirit.

Jude 20 NLT

VALUES

Do not be conformed to this world,
but be transformed by the renewal of your
mind, that by testing you may discern
what is the will of God, what is good
and acceptable and perfect.

Romans 12:2 ESV

Let us behave decently. Clothe yourselves with
the Lord Jesus Christ, and do not think about
how to gratify the desires of the flesh.

Romans 13:13-14 NIV

Values

Do not love this world nor the things
it offers you, for when you love the world,
you do not have the love of the
Father in you. Anyone who does what
pleases God will live forever.

1 John 2:15, 17 NLT

"So in everything, do to others what you
would have them do to you, for this sums
up the Law and the Prophets."

Matthew 7:12 NIV

He's already made it plain how to live,
what to do, what God is looking for in men
and women. It's quite simple: Do what is fair
and just to your neighbor, be compassionate
and loyal in your love, and don't take yourself
too seriously – take God seriously.

Micah 6:8 MSG

Values

Treat everyone you meet with dignity.
Love your spiritual family.
Revere God. Respect the government.

1 Peter 2:17 MSG

Submit yourselves therefore to God. Resist
the devil, and he will flee from you. Draw near
to God, and He will draw near to you.
Cleanse your hands, you sinners, and purify
your hearts, you double-minded.

James 4:7-8 ESV

Jesus said to the crowd, "If any of you
wants to be My follower, you must
turn from your selfish ways, take up
your cross daily, and follow Me."

Luke 9:23 NLT

Values

Let there be no filthiness nor foolish talk
nor crude joking, which are out of place,
but instead let there be thanksgiving.

Ephesians 5:4 ESV

Let steadfastness have its full effect,
that you may be perfect and
complete, lacking in nothing.

James 1:4 ESV

Every good gift and every perfect gift is
from above, coming down from the Father
of lights with whom there is no variation
or shadow due to change.

James 1:17 ESV

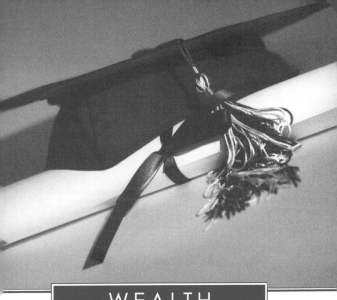

WEALTH

Remember the LORD your God, for it is He
who gives you the ability to produce wealth.

Deuteronomy 8:18 NIV

Honor the LORD with your wealth and with
the best part of everything you produce.
Then He will fill your barns with grain,
and your vats will overflow with good wine.

Proverbs 3:9-10 NLT

Wealth

God will meet all your needs according to
the riches of His glory in Christ Jesus.

Philippians 4:19 NIV

Teach those who are rich in this world not
to be proud and not to trust in their money,
which is so unreliable. Their trust should
be in God, who richly gives us all
we need for our enjoyment.

1 Timothy 6:17 NLT

God can pour on the blessings in astonishing
ways so that you're ready for anything and
everything, more than just ready to
do what needs to be done.

2 Corinthians 9:8 MSG

Wealth

The love of money is the root of all kinds
of evil. And some people, craving money,
have wandered from the true faith and
pierced themselves with many sorrows.

1 Timothy 6:10 NLT

Each one must give as he has decided in his
heart, not reluctantly or under compulsion,
for God loves a cheerful giver.

2 Corinthians 9:7 ESV

Give generously to the poor, not grudgingly,
for the LORD your God will bless
you in everything you do.

Deuteronomy 15:10 NLT

Wealth

It is a good thing to receive wealth
from God and the good health to enjoy it.
To enjoy your work and accept your lot in
life – this is indeed a gift from God.

Ecclesiastes 5:19 NLT

Don't love money; be satisfied
with what you have.

Hebrews 13:5 NLT

Those who trust in the LORD
will lack no good thing.

Psalm 34:10 NLT

WORK

"Let your good deeds shine out
for all to see, so that everyone
will praise your heavenly Father."

Matthew 5:16 NLT

Whatever you do, do well. For when you
go to the grave, there will be no work or
planning or knowledge or wisdom.

Ecclesiastes 9:10 NLT

Work

God, your God, will bless you
in all your work.

Deuteronomy 24:19 MSG

Work willingly at whatever you do,
as though you were working for
the Lord rather than for people.

Colossians 3:23 NLT

My dear brothers and sisters, be strong and
immovable. Always work enthusiastically
for the Lord, for you know that nothing
you do for the Lord is ever useless.

1 Corinthians 15:58 NLT

Work

Make a careful exploration
of who you are and the work
you have been given,
and then sink yourself into that.
Don't be impressed with yourself.
Don't compare yourself with others.
Each of you must take responsibility
for doing the creative best
you can with your own life.

Galatians 6:4-5 MSG

"His master said to him, 'Well done,
good and faithful servant. You have been
faithful over a little; I will set you over much.
Enter into the joy of your master.'"

Matthew 25:21 ESV

Work

Whatever you do, in word or
deed, do everything in the name of
the Lord Jesus, giving thanks to God
the Father through Him.

Colossians 3:17 ESV

The LORD your God will bless you in all your
harvest and in all the work of your hands,
and your joy will be complete.

Deuteronomy 16:15 NIV

Make every effort to confirm your
calling and election. For if you do
these things, you will never stumble.

2 Peter 1:10 NIV

Work

Put God in charge of your work,
then what you've planned will take place.

Proverbs 16:3 msg

A Graduate's Prayer

Dear Lord, as I look toward the future
Bright hope conducts this prayer,
For I know the plans You have for me
Were wrought with divine care.

Your Word will be a lamp for me,
A guide to light my way,
A solid place to set my feet,
A compass when I stray.

May I live my life to praise You,
Not for fortune, nor for fame,
May everything I say and do
Bring glory to Your name.

Planted by Your living streams
I'll delight in all Your ways,
Hidden by Your sheltering wings
With new mercies for each day.

Dear Lord, show me Your favor,
At all times keep me blessed,
May Your face ever shine upon me,
With peace and perfect rest.
Amen.

- Mary Fairchild -